EARTHSONG

A poetic autobiography

A true life experience of fear and hope

by

Hans Lohse

ISBN-13: 978-1461031642
ISBN-10: 1461031648
BISAC: Biography & Autobiography / General

ACKNOWLEDGMENTS

I would like to gratefully acknowledge the
inspirational energy
advice and encouragement
I received writing my life story

Kristin "Marlena" DiErrico
My partner in life and the best editor in the world

Sandy and Marilena Vaccaro
The Smart Graphics designers for the powerful book cover
and so much invaluable computer help

Kathleen Marszycki
For showing me how to organize the English language

Linda Sacha
For her insightful suggestions and her bountiful love

Justin Vood Good
For writing the eloquent book description
and for his spirited musicianship

To all my friends who influenced me
from the past and the present
who walked worked and played
laughed and cried with me
I acknowledge your presence in my life
with gratitude and love

You all made it possible
as a collective being

CHAPTER ONE
EARLY MEMORIES

SEE BEAUTY AND HEAR MUSIC
IN EVERYTHING

The Little People

When I choose my parents and their location
to enter this world
it is a small town in northern Germany
neighboring a coal mine
showing off tall brick smoke stacks
spewing black smoke and smelly particles
that settle over everything

It is the first day of an ice cold December
1938

June Bug

I wonder where my father is

My mother tearfully saddens
"Your father is far away
fighting the war in Russia"

She puts me on her lap and sings to me

Maikaefer flieg
Dein Vater ist im Krieg
Deine Mutter ist in Pommerland
Pommerland ist abgebrannt
Maikaefer flieg

June Bug fly far
Your father fights the War
Your mother came from Pommerland
Pommerland is burning down
June bug fly far

Mother

A seamstress
She had given birth to my brother two years earlier

I am "Buebchen"
"Muttersoehnchen"
My mothers little son
she had hoped for a girl she could dress

I love to wrap my arms around her
Kisses
Sharing her pleasures and laughter
so little
so innocent
so in love

Running from danger
searching for our little hands
She shelters and provides
cradles our heads to calm our fears
sings to us in her clear angel voice

As I grow
she abruply ends her affection
I feel lost
lonely
I ache for her love

She aches for her love

Spring Awakening

There is great excitement and stirring celebration

Blood red banners and flags
embossed with black swastikas everywhere
hanging out of windows and doors
draped over walls and fences
carried and waved in joyful dedication
by men women and children

Colorful marching bands with rousing sounds parade the streets
followed by crowds of overjoyed people

The masses raise their hands in unison
hysterically roaring

Heil Hitler! Heil – Heil – Heil!

I am a small fragile little boy
celebrating innocently
the birthday of our beloved Fuehrer

German Anthem

At night
in the center of the city
music plays
This time with different musicians
producing a sharp startling metallic sound
iron cleats fastened to the heels of their shiny black leather boots

Clack clack! Clack clack! Clack clack!
They march smartly stepping high
arms swinging in a precise arrogant gait
Clack clack! Clack clack! Clack clack!

They form rows
facing the throng
gathering for the rally in the square
torch flames dance in a sea of uniformed faces

I cling to my mother's arm
shivering with excitement and fright

Everyone roars the German Anthem
"Deutschland Deutschland ueber alles
ueber alles in der Welt....."

Attack

In the middle of the night
penetrating howling sirens make us run for shelter

People frightfully pushing and shoving
into the dark opening of the underground bunker

In the concrete vault
I huddle close to my mother and brother
Waiting
waiting in fearful silence
anticipating the attacks

First there is a humming sound
like the chanting of a prayer circle
intensifying with the frightening and hissing sounds of metal
bursting through the air with ever increasing speed
exploding into deadly fire

The earth shakes
the naked light bulb hangs from a wire
dancing with the rhythm of explosions
until it pops it's fragile shell

We are in total darkness
cowering on the wet and cold dirt floor
shielding ourselves from objects falling out of blackness
holding our breath against sickening gases
suddenly the door blasts into pieces
In panic and fearful desperation we push to the outside

The city is burning around us
shouts for loved ones
cries for help

We run

Panic

The train has not moved for hours
people crowd inside
bursting outside
onto platforms
doorsteps and rooftops
It smells of rotten fish

We lose my brother in the chaos of pushing bodies
mother is rushing up and down outside the train
panic stricken
calling out my brother's name
Suddenly the train begins to move
I press my frightened face against the cold hard glass

Slowly
the train gains speed
the scale of the burning red and black city
disappears in the distance

Cold and alone
at the next train station
the conductor takes me to the waiting hall
filled with people
slouched on hard wooden stools and benches
resting their heads
on wooden tables
sleeping on top of their belongings
waiting for a train

There is free ox-tail soup

The Dream

Listening to the humming of approaching bombers
I push my shaking body against my mother
cover my head with my jacket
close my eyes tightly
hope in desperation for everything to go away
change into something magical
as I know from fairytales

Determined to escape this frightful reality
it happens
a vision appears

Transported on a mythical kite
gliding effortlessly through blue sky
toward a distant green mountain
tall swaying trees
invite me to come closer

My curious mind imagines shimmering grasses singing with the wind
colorful exotic birds sailing and diving through the air
guiding me gently closer to the mountain
to a small enchanting castle with peaked roof towers
reaching out to the summer sky
embracing me

I hold on to this soothing vision as long as I can
hold on to this magical wonderful journey from darkness into light
as if my life depends on it

Where before there was fear
now there is hope

The Painting

My small body is pressed against the window
by the force of people pushing into the train car
happy to secure this place
holding on steadfast
I am determined not to be pushed away

I see outside from this position
escaping the dark smelly wrestling interior of the train
eager to drink as much of the view as I can

What I see will forever be engraved in my mind's eye

The City of Hamburg reveals its dark and sad silhouette
before a spectacular golden sunset

Some buildings are standing unharmed
but most are reduced to despair
destroyed by bombs and fire
leaving broken facades of masonry walls with empty holes
where glazed windows used to be

I imagine the people that lived in these buildings
mothers fathers sisters brothers grandparents
Did the bombs kill them
Were they able to escape

Pressing my face against the cold glass
the train unexpectedly begins to move

In the sun's golden light
Hundreds of "Fesselballons" danced restlessly in the air
slowly disappearing behind the ruins
of a once lively City

Mother Earth

The train comes to a screeching halt
a demanding voice shouts

"Rauss Rauss Rauss"
"Out Out Out"

Mother grabs my brother and I
pushing with the hurried and scared crowd to the exit
jumping from the platform into the dark
running and falling down the steep bank
into the nearby forest

Low flying speed fighters attack the train with splitting machine gun fire
swooshing over our heads with ear deafening noise and speed

Then there is silence

We hover in fear
afraid to move
I feel hot burning urine running down my shivering legs

The airplanes approach again
with their frightening sounds
and their spitting fires

I press my body close to the ground
my face into the dirt
crawl with my mind
into the earth

The Sea

Listening to the rousing sounds of the ocean waves in the distance
my mother brother and I walk through the grey misty dusk
of the quiet late afternoon
toward the endlessly calling waters
breathing eagerly the healing aroma of the sea

It is the first time we experience this mystical gift
we let the rhythm of the sea penetrate deep inside us
Our bare feet embrace the gentle cool sand
and with each careful step
a magical sight unfolds before our bedazzled eyes

Through the settling moist fog
the sea appears in constant rolling shimmering motion
pushed and pulled by nature's force
rising falling and calling in wild excitement
crushing toward the shore and breaking into white foam
seductively kissing our naked feet

We see a woman kneeling
her dark haired head bowed to the earth
her hands folded in prayer
incoming waves surround her naked motionless body
staring at her in silence
she is unaware of our presence

After a seemingly endless time she raises her head and arms
toward the horizon of the sea
standing in a straight and determined position
she walks without hesitation
into the grasping waters
embracing her body
carrying it further and further away
from the safety of the shore

We see her dark head bouncing up and down
diminishing and disappearing in the gray horizon

"Will she come back?" I ask my mother
Her eyes are filled with tears
she does not answer

Uncle Fritz

My uncle Fritz is one of the lucky men
He survived the war without losing a limb

As he buries his uniform in the back yard
a British soldier shoots him dead

He falls into the hole
on top of his uniform

Helpless

I can hear the horseshoes from far away
Iron wagon wheels turning on cobblestones

I see the horses head
stretched forward
close to the ground
pulling a heavy wagonload of coal

Ice has settled on the road
the horse slips
frightened desperate and confused

The man jerks on the reins
struggling to gain control
using his wooden stick mercilessly
with force and anger
beating the bony horse to the ground

I see the pain in the horses eyes
Sadly I watch
frozen
shivering
helpless

Schwarzer Mann

With the exception of his eyes
everything is covered with black soot
the formal top hat
the long armed jacket
his pants billowing away from his body
black wooden clogs cover his bare feet

Over his shoulder he carries an iron ring
attached to an iron ball and steel brushes

He appears high up
on ridges of steep clay tiled roofs
balancing with naked feet

We stretch our necks with open mouths and watch in awe
knowing that it brings good fortune
to see a chimney sweep

The Gift

" He is blessed with an angels voice"
mother proudly proclaims
to the neighboring women and children
gathered to listen to my singing

I jump from her lap
stand up in a firm and brave position
encouraged by the reward of loving praises
I open my mouth
singing from my heart and soul

I find new strength in every note
without fear
without control
I sing the song of the moment
improvised
out of nowhere
pouring effortlessly through me

I don't know the source of this music
all I feel is tranquil safe and strong
I trust this magic moment

Hope

The GI's have settled down in their corrugated metal huts

They drive fascinating cars and trucks
they smell of gasoline and smoke

They are adored by frightened and hungry children
they are loved by lonely and tired women

They bring us food
nylons
cigarettes
jazz
hope
and sweet chocolate
Sweet chocolate for the kid who can say "fucking bastard"

They roar with laughter
Fucking Bastards

The Feeding

Every morning all the children are standing in line
skinny and anxious
holding our abused aluminum cans in one hand
spoons in the other

Greeted by cheerful hurrahs
the GIs arrive in their open camouflage jeeps and trucks
talking loud and constant
always laughing

They unload large cans filled with thick oatmeal or pea soup
They fill our cans displaying curious looks and friendly smiles
They speak to us in a language we cannot understand
it must be encouraging
their faces are bright and happy

We like Americans
we are happy to see them
we are grateful they feed us

The Banana

He rises in front of me in his towering presence
a huge dark colored man
leather boots tied almost all the way to his knees
his oversized body bursting out of his uniform

The biggest black fist I have ever seen
is holding a banana
reaching out to me with a broad friendly grin
strange and foreign with a chocolate face
exposing lots of shiny white teeth

It is the first banana I have ever tasted
the first act of love I have received from a man

Father

The train stops at the station
smelling of black coal
hot iron and steam

A handful of tired and dirty men in uniform
painfully climb down the steps
and walk slowly toward the gate

A strange man limps in my direction
two crutches pressed under his arms hold most of his body weight
his neck disappearing in a dark brown ripped army coat
revealing only one leg

He calls out my name
I turn and run away as fast as I can

He often cries
his face marked with memories of war
his spirit broken
he has a need to show off his wounds

For him the world is Godless

He never talks about the horror

I learn much later in life
his need for comfort and love
was even greater than mine

Settling

Cramped into one room
a coal burning cooking stove heats the space
and hot water for bathing in a tin tub

Under a metal top table
a bucket to wash dishes

My parents bed and the couch I share with my brother
is separated by a fabric curtain

In a corner next to the window
a half round rusted cast iron wall mounted sink
serves as a urinal

We store coal and potatoes in the cellar

A steep concrete stair with an iron pipe railing
leads to a dark exterior court
passing wired covered wooden cages
filled with hyperactive rabbits
stalls with smelly grunting pigs
and curious goats

A slippery mud path
leads to the outhouse
I light a candle
open the wooden lid
awful smells
spiders
flies
no paper

Family

My father is plagued with nightmares
my mother comforts him

He drinks alcohol to calm his pain

When he comes home late at night
hoping for comfort
they abusively argue

I hide with my brother
under the darkness of the blanket
in the safety of dreams

Grandfather

First there is a distant drumbeat
not a dancing beat
a marching beat

Bum babum bum babum bum babum

I run toward the sound with anticipation and excitement
the band appears in all its glorious shining gold and flashing silver
marching to a big demanding sound

The music is loud and awesome
the brassy tubas with their ship's horn sound
the big bass drums pounding one monotonous beat
Bum babum bum babum bum babum

The little snare drums rattle like machine gun fire
Rata tat tat rata tatat rata tatat

Shrill shiny pipes and flutes whistle
demanding attention to the melody

My grandfather proudly leads the coal miners marching band
swinging his shimmering baton precisely to the marching beat
He is a tall handsome man with a seductive smirk
an elegant mustache and a twinkle in his eyes
He makes sure that he is loved by women
He has fathered thirteen children
with the exception of two
he lost them all to Hitler's war

In the end he lost his mind
they found him in the woods
hanging from a tree

Volksempfaenger

Great celebration
we are able to buy a radio
a "Volksempfaenger"
a receiver for the masses

It has the appearance of a small simple sculptured bust
a round shaven head
sitting on two undulating shoulders
centered by a burlap covered hole
a metallic sounding speaker behind
two black knobs for controls

Radio "Suchdienst"
The station monotonously announces all day long
names of missing persons
dates
residence unknown

At night I listen eagerly to "Hoerspiele" (Hear plays)
fantasizing about different worlds
creating visions to spoken words

I learn to love classical music
pressing my ear against the small speaker
closer to the source
so many beautiful sounds
"Freude schoener Goetterfunke........"
people singing with conviction from their heart and soul

I cry

The Landlady

She is our landlady
her name is Alma
strong and angry

Richard her husband is her daily victim

One day she smashes his head with an iron frying pan
pushing him down the stairs

I see him falling
poor Richard

We are all afraid of Alma

The Landlady's Daughter

She is much older and very beautiful

She shows me a sizable porcelain figure
in the form of a pig with a slot on top
She promises to fill it each day I work for her with ten pennies

I work hard and eager
tending to the animals and gardens
until I lose count of days and pennies

Over the years she never mentions the piggy bank again
I never ask

Schlachtefest

Desperate squealing cries
I sit up straight in bed

I bundle up against the icy cold
sitting in the dark enclosed courtyard
on top of the concrete stairs
peaking through the iron balusters
below me
a circus arena

Men struggle to restrain a strong big pig
eventually succeeding
wrestling the pig to the ground
one holds a steel bolt
another swings a hammer
cries explode into the air
the pig runs wild in circles
a steel bolt in his forehead
collapsing from exhaustion

I sit frozen
watching the pig being cut in half
white and red
stretched out on the barn door
to be cooked in the kettle

Neighbors show up with their aluminum cans

School

We are a sad weary bunch of boys
Undernourished
wrapped in dirty patched clothing
diverse in age and separated from the girls
hunched over from memories of fear
assembled in a makeshift classroom
forever waiting for our teacher to arrive

Learning is new to us
we play in streets
bombed out buildings
sun drenched cornfields

We are always waiting for a new teacher
using the time to be rowdy and restless

The older boys teach the younger how to masturbate

Teacher 1

She walks into the classroom

Everyone roars with laughter
pointing fingers
making fun of her

She is a short woman
more wide than tall
hunchbacked

Her face grows dark stringy hair above her upper lip
we call her "Mieze"
she reminds us of a fat cat

She demands unsuccessfully
to calm our boyish judgments
She leaves tearfully
never to return

We wait again

Teacher 2

He is an angry man
forcefully trying to discipline us
his method quick and successful
he is feared by all

He makes us sit up straight
eyes on the blackboard
both hands stretched out on the table
he slowly walks from the rear of the classroom
down the aisle
hitting our hands randomly and unexpectedly
with a feared wooden stick
leaving us with painful swollen bloody fingers

I can still hear the hissing sound of the wooden stick
rushing by my ear
the cry of pain
the sobbing

I remember learning nothing except
sadness
fear
and anger

Teacher 3

Proudly he states
the reason he survived the war
was because he rode his bicycle up hills
adding stones to his pockets
to build up his muscles

He largely dislikes our fragile appearance
wanting us to be bodily fit
My thin body does not resemble Aryan perfection
He enjoys exposing my shortcomings
leaving me feeling shameful and sad

He demands us to raise our hand
waiting for him to ask us to speak
This is a strict order
I painfully try to obey

Holding back my desperate urge
to go to the bathroom
he ignores my request
I can no longer hold it
Panic stricken
I feel the warm fluid soaking my pants
running down my legs into my shoes
onto the wooden floor

Standing close to the warm drying radiator
avoiding the grins from my classmates

I feel deep paralyzing shame

Herr Kreutzer

Our part time music teacher
with a wounded and distorted face
hugs his violin between shoulder and chin
we see his pain

His bow glides over iron strings like satin
fingers climb the scale with pounding speed
his upper body twists and turns
saliva spitting from his mouth
with the passion of his music
his violin is aching

In the front row
looking up
I am fascinated and inspired

Growing Up

Summers are good to us

Rowdy boys and girls roam through golden cornfields
soaking our pale skinny bodies in the bright warming sunlight
discovering our sexuality

Swimming in gravel pits
bizarre steel sculptures look out at us
reminders of the war

There are plenty of apple and cherry trees to climb and eat from
The farmer's fields provide us generously with beets peas and carrots
bushes full of wild berries for dessert

Using found objects
the toys we play with are improvised
we construct stilts from tree branches and broom sticks

We search for wheels and scrap wood
to build cars for wild soap car derbies
using the cars to collect paper and scrap metal
selling for pennies

Shops open
we stay in line to purchase
horsemeat
gray flour
brown sugar
and watery green milk

The Border

It is a short walk to the next town
to play in the water of the gentle brook
the dividing line between West and East

Russian soldiers erect wooden watchtowers
I innocently wave to them
They shout back

They plow a wide and endless strip of land
planting field mines
between two high dense wooden walls
with barbed wire on top

The neighboring town disappears from sight
only the church steeple is visible

Brother

My older brother
chooses not to play with me

His talents are physical
he excels in running
bicycle racing
and winter sports

Turning fifteen
he leaves home
peddles his self made bicycle throughout Europe

He joins the Merchant Marines
and adventurously travels the world

Wanting to be like him
I place myself in his shadow
longing for his strength and courage

My strength and courage comes from music

The Boxing Match

I feel the painful blows of his fist to my face
my vision blurred
knees wobbling
I am held up and pushed forward by a circle of children
shouting encouragements

I know this match is hopeless for me
The Bully is Big
Strong
Stupid

I am being sacrificed

Guided by the strength of my voice
I let out a scream of horror
stopping everyone in motion
that split second of surprise my small fist shoots out with all its might
straight to his unprotected nose
blood splashing all around
fear in his eyes
he runs away

Trying to calm my shivering body
I don't want to repeat that aggressive act again

They celebrate me like a hero

Willy

He is confused about everything

His mother has to call him several times
in her outstretched high pitched voice
before Willy notices that the call is meant for him

He is constantly busy
pulling buggars out of his oversized nose
rolling them between the tips of his fingers
just dry enough
to chew them like gum

His father is missing in action

Rudy

Everyone calls him "Klotzkopf"
someone with a wooden block in his head

He adopts the behavior of a steam train
his skinny arms bent at his waist move back and forth
in alternate motions
his feet inspired
he shuffles to the left and shuffles to the right
his mouth spitting sounds of steam
he rarely stops
he never speaks

Sitting next to him
on a train
a bomb
killed his parents

Isolde

She is the oldest among the children
showing off her developed breasts

She grabs me
pressing her big wet lips against my mouth

Ashamed of my excitement
I run away
hoping for a next time

Siegrid

We are a small group of neighborhood children
hovering on the bank of the railroad track
waiting in silent tension for the coal train to appear

It is a chilly winter night
biting icy wind and anticipation make us shiver
my frozen hand tightens around the empty burlap sack
hoping to be filled with black coal

We know the train will slow its speed
come to a screeching halt just before the red signal
giving us the time we need to rush up the steep bank
quickly climb the loaded wagon
fill our sacks with coal
throw them to the ground
collect the bounty
and run into the safety of the night
It is a routine we practiced often

We can hear how far away the train is by pressing our ear to the iron track
tonight the train is late
Nearby barking of feared German Shepherds intensify our anxieties

Finally the train appears around the bend
I jump onto the wagon
fill my sack with coal
The train does not come to a complete stop
I see the red signal changing to green
the train picks up speed and I blindly throw my bag into the darkness
there is a piercing cry of pain from below

I cannot jump anymore
I dig myself into the black coal to shield my shivering body
The next town is eight kilometers away
a cold long and lonely walk home

The coal sack I threw from the wagon
landed directly on Siegrid's head
she has a concussion and stitches
I go often to visit her in the hospital
They say that she will be the one I marry

The Gate Keeper

We love to kneel next to the railroad tracks
waiting for the next train to steam around the corner
closer and closer
We place our pennies on the track just in time
to watch the iron train wheels smash the copper flat

We feel on top of the world
walking down the track to the friendly gate keeper

Dressed in his soldier uniform
he struggles to open the gate
forcing the crank

Saluting all passing trains
he raises his left arm straight to the sky

His right arm is missing

The Accordion

Walking uphill to the city square
he walks in front of me
lifting his body on wooden crutches pressed securely under his arms

With each step my father's crutches find a secure place among the cobblestones
His upper body falls into the support of his crutches
pushing his one leg into a swing
repeating this maneuver
like the pendulum of my grandfather's clock

Every summer the circus rolls in with colorful wagons
exotic animals
breathtaking acrobats
waving proudly

The circus band is placed dominantly on top the curtained entrance
overlooking the ring of fascinations
I love to listen to their music
I want to be one of them

At the end of the city square
perched among connected buildings from the middle ages
a toy store appears
a happy series of bells above the low entrance door welcome us
the squeaky old wood floor smells freshly oiled

The store is filled with wooden carved animals
miniature trains running endlessly in circles
maneuvering through fairytale landscapes
dollhouses I want to live in
puppet theatres I want to act in
paper lanterns and noise makers

Among all these glittering treasures
my father hands me
a small shiny accordion

It is the happiest day in my life

Tarzan

A great event happens
The first Movie Theatre opens
admission is pennies and some coal to heat the stove
The hall is packed with curious people
staring at a big white screen in exciting anticipation

"Tarzan the Ape Man" with German subtitles
Olympic swimmer Johnny Weissmuller as Tarzan
Maureen O'Sullivan as Jane Parker
The first and only English words I understand
"Me Tarzan – you Jane"

I watch him swing and swim
listen to his incredible yodel
he is free
half naked
living my dream in a self made tree house
far away

He is my hero
he makes me want to swim
I join a sports club
to train for swimming and diving competitions

The Competition

My mother teaches me how to use the Singer sewing machine

Two simple canvas triangles are stitched together serving as a bathing suit
tightened at the waist by a string

Standing in a crouched position on top of the starting block
tensely waiting for the sound of the whistle
I feel my self made string lose its tension

The whistle sounds
I frantically try to tighten the stubborn string
jumping in a forward outstretched motion
forcefully into the water
my suit decides to let go of me

Under the water
I search for it
to cover my nakedness
Roaring laughter from the spectators above

This is my first and only experience with competitive sports

Shame

I stare into nothingness
blood rushing to my head
out of control
my face turns into the red of a ripe tomato

My feelings of insecurity and weakness are exposed
to two young women sitting across from me
on hard wooden benches
riding the train home from school

The pretty women smile at me with comfortable superiority
the blood in my head wants to burst
in panic I reach for my book
open it and hold it close to cover my face
turning the pages
pretending to read

"Excuse me," one of the women said with a giggle
"your book is upside down"

Work

I am convinced I am not High School material
leaving my mother with painful disappointment
me with burdening guilt

I like to work with my hands

The salt mine is hard work
especially the night shift
hot salty and noisy
We face a huge mound of raw densely packed salt
and scrape the heavy salt onto the conveyer belt
If there is too little or too much
a noisy horn sounds

Huge steel tanks are heated by a network of iron pipes
extracting salt from water
Regularly these pipes get covered with a hard salty crust
which needs to be chiseled off

We strip down to our underwear
slip our feet into protective leather boots
cover our naked bodies with large heavy paper bags
protecting us from constant hot water drips

Entering the tank through a small manhole
we hammer and chisel with aching backs in unbearable heat
My skinny body does not tolerate this work for long
I need to find another job

Selling nails in a hardware store is too monotonous
I get fired for lack of sincerity and commitment

I dig trenches and install culverts
at least it's outside

Inspiration

Weekends I play my accordion
in a quartet of musicians
people like what they hear
they dance

We sing political satire
poking fun of anything undemocratic and inhumane

We play cheerful waltzes
rousing polkas
slow and romantic songs for the American soldiers
loud rock and roll for the restless and curious German youth

American music is our inspiration
We listen in awe
Elvis Presley Bill Haley and His Comets
Nat King Cole Billy Holiday Miles Davis John Coltrane Charlie Parker
Louis Armstrong
Ella
on and on
over and over
We sing the words from memory
unaware of their meaning

We eagerly imitate Americans
chew gum
smoke
spit
wanting to be like them

Early Fifties

"Four of us"
Name of the band

Saxophone Player

We know little about him
He is not able to pee when others are present
He lives in a housing complex
hitchhikes to gigs

Guitar Player

He is the most handsome
His head full of big black greasy hair
Women fall for him
He wants to go on the road
wants me to go with him

Drum Player

He is the only one with means of transportation
He drives a BMW motorcycle
His chin holds on to his base drum strapped to his chest
while I....

Accordion Player

climb onto the back seat
accordion strapped to my back
holding on to everything

Peter

His artistic talent attracts me

Next to the hardware store
he works as a window dresser for a clothing shop
his window displays are enchanting
he is a celebrity in town

His mother waits in vain
for her husband to return home from war

Missing in action
she declares him dead
able to marry another

He wants to apply to art school
he urges me to do the same

Peter is my best friend

The Burden

It is a strenuous walk uphill to Grandmother
She lives in a home smelling of old things
at the edge of the Elm Forest
She speaks with a heavy Ukrainian accent

Sitting in her comfortable armchair in front of the window
she longingly looks out into the forest
Her lap is covered with a warm woolen blanket
her body is in constant motion
backward and forward
steady like the ticking of a clock

She offers me tasty wrinkled apples from a box
stored under her bed
Another box
is filled with all kinds of strings ropes pins and paper bags
"I save everything
I never know when I might need it"
She is a wise woman

She stops her constant rocking motion
looks at me sadly
takes my hand
"You will have to carry the burden of your Father's history
and when you are in pain
go into the woods
to find yourself"

Letting go of me
she continues her rocking

I visit her often

Hannelore

She is sixteen years young
very attractive
lifted up straight by fashionable high heeled shoes
she notices no one

She takes the same train to a neighboring city morning and night
She walks the same road home
I always manage to walk behind her at a respectful distance

One rainy evening
I gather my courage
ask to carry her umbrella
from then on we walk home together
I invite her to jazz concerts

She fled with her family
in the dark of night
from Communist occupied Germany
through the mine fields
to the free West

We begin to see each other more often
and soon marry

I love her like a sister
she loves me like a brother
I am restlessly crazy
she wants me to be perfect

I want to be wild

The Draft

March 1959
A dark day
I receive my draft notice from the "Kreiswehrersatzamt"
The Germans are forming an army again

My memories are of a lost and painful childhood
I am not made for soldier duty
I don't want to learn how to shoot cannons or drop bombs

I desire to be free
ache to discover the vast world
see beautiful cities
meet foreign people
I am curious about life's offerings

The Art Academy is accepting talented students
fine arts
visual arts
architecture

Freedom from the draft

Great celebration
I am accepted
I begin to study the art of architecture

Professor Wolfgang Stadelmeier

He is my mentor
my hero
his place is right next to Tarzan
He owns a sleek elegant white French Citroen
a sensuous driving experience with fashionable purple cushy seats
He drives his car with excessive speed across Germany's Autobahn
teaches creativity with gusto and charm

We all love him unconditionally
The young men dress like him
The young women adore him
Some are his lover

Gently and humorously he guides us in our failures
celebrates generously our successes
encourages us to seek the unknown

We drive in chartered buses throughout Europe
witnessing the unharmed treasures of art and architecture
drowning in beauty and wine

We listen to jazz from America
the Classics from Europe
reading Goethe Nietzsche Sartre and Beckett
watch New Wave French movies
smoking cigarettes endlessly
passionately discussing philosophy
we feel intellectual

Seductively he preaches
"Be inspired by nature and life just the way it is
Be aware of your senses at all times
Connect with your feelings
Work with your hands
Welcome all changes"

He lives in a small castle in the wine hills of Stuttgart
overlooking the shimmering city below
He is living my dream

The Lecture

The Dean posts an unexpected announcement
students are to assemble
to view a documentary film
Our tensions and expectations increase
walking noisily into the auditorium
we take our seats
There are no announcements
lights dim to complete darkness

What we are about to see and hear
for the first time in our youthful lives
profoundly changes us
fills us with horrifying revulsion and pain
leaving us with unbearable shame and guilt

We witness in graphic black and white
the Horror of the Holocaust

We watch in disbelief and exhaustion
the systematic murder of the Jewish people
Horrifying images of men women and children
stripped of their belongings
robbed of their dignity
shot at close range
Hurled into mass graves by iron men and machines without feelings

How could this happen
Why Why Why

Where can we place our turmoil
Our Rage
Why have these horrific crimes been shrouded in silence

We walk slowly and shaky out of the auditorium
unable to look at each other
We cannot make the horrors an object of discussion

For us collective guilt becomes a living reality
We become Germany's angry generation

The Interview

The Professor arranges my first job interview

I carry his encouragement
displaying my youthful confidence
as an attractive receptionist announces my arrival

I enter the luxurious office
Spectacular views of the City of Stuttgart
I am in awe

An overweight body bends over a large working table
crowded with plans and models
"I have to do everything myself"
he complains
"I can not find good people"

He inspects my portfolio
to my delight
offers me the job
After revealing the small salary I am to receive
surprisingly I hear myself say
"No wonder you can't find good people"

His response is swift and determined
his mouth foaming
He stands up in a straight position stretching out his arm
pointing his finger toward my frightened face and shouts
"Rauss"! (Out)

I am devastated
ashamed
angry
and without a job

Rebellion

We detest anything regimented and in uniform
rules and regulations
flags and banners
we hate police
the army

We learn how quickly patriotism can turn into racist nationalism

Our anger turns against ourselves
we become wild and reckless
chain smoke potent French cigarettes
drink excessively
drive fast brand new sports cars
smash them against trees
roll them down steep banks
in the dark of night

We are always running
away from order
responsibility
authority

Escape

1968
A tumultuous year

The authorities are closing in
It is time to run

This time I am running far away
across the Atlantic Ocean
to unknown adventures
to a country I only know from movies

Hannelore and I say goodbye
making desperate love in our fear

A friend races me in his silver Porsche
on winding roads through the darkness of night
to reach the border of Switzerland

The airplane leaves Geneva
scheduled to land in New York
I sink into my seat
exhausted and excited

new hope

Arrival

What I see

appearing below me
breaking through the fast moving clouds
takes my breath away

A massive landscape of monumental buildings
almost tall enough to touch the airplane
a seemingly never ending mass
of concrete
steel and glass
constantly changing shape and form

I have never seen such a grandiose dance of architecture
I am mesmerized by its starkness and motion
I can't resist this exciting mess of a city

New York

Once on the ground
I am swallowed
by packs of people
pushing carts full of baggage
shouting in foreign languages
looking for direction

The line is divided
one for citizens
the other for foreigners
Unable to speak the language
I anxiously consult my German-English dictionary
"Are you a visitor"
"Yes I am a visitor"

I slowly decipher a sign reading
We hope you enjoy your stay in America

I want to stay forever

CHAPTER TWO

A NEW LIFE

TO ALL MY RELATIONS

Free

No one is looking at me
I see the flashy reflection of the city
in their eyes and glasses

Everything is pulsating
constantly moving and changing
Awesome noises and sounds
like a huge unrehearsed orchestra
trying to get in tune before a grand symphony

The city swallows me
I walk without destination or direction
fascinated by enormous neon billboards
larger than life figures
advertising movies
plays
goods and sex

All my belongings are in a small bag
I have no cares
no fear
no doubt

At this moment
I am alone
Free

First Night

I find a room at a YMCA
the only place I know to go
A stuffy tiny space
big enough for a bed in one corner
an old beat up dresser
a plastic covered chair against the wall

A large cast iron radiator is in front of the window
exposing a dreary view to a brick façade
The window does not open
it probably has not been open for years
The radiator steams in harmony with the aggressive noises of the city

I lie naked on the smelly bed
as I watch roaches escape the flashing city lights
reflected on the ceiling

My first night in America
curious
exciting
hot
adventurous
full of lust

1968

The Greyhound bus hustles through the hectic city streets
confronted by detours and stop lights

Through the window I see endless miles of cemeteries
densely filled with monumental ornamented gravestones

How many people live in this large eccentric city
How many died

The bus passes by never ending rows
abandoned and burned out buildings
unoccupied and crumbling structures

Why are so many people
begging and sleeping in alleys and on street corners
Why are so many black
Why is what I see so dirty
ugly sad and full of tension

This is not the America I remember from movies
these pictures are frightfully real

American cities are burning

Christa

Christa chose to run away from the war to the United States
only to be swept away by a handsome charming Italian
who likes to gamble
betting his belongings and life away
They have four beautiful children

She takes me in

I help with the chores
bringing up a quartet of little German-Italian-Americans

Late at night I watch and laugh with Johnny Carson
and his colorful guests
This is how I learn to speak English

A New Country

I am eager for adventure
to adopt other customs
meet new friends

My rebellious spirit feels at home
protesting wars and injustice

I am now in a country that helped liberate Germany
America
Country of Dreams
Freedom
Hope

In the center of the city
there are marching bands
arousing sounds
People wave and salute the American flag
placing hands on their hearts
pledging allegiance with passionate conviction
displaying pride and superiority

AMERICA
NUMBER ONE

DEUTSCHLAND
UEBER ALLES

Love Boat

Hannelore is finally coming to America
It has been almost two years
since I left her in fear and confusion

I can see her approaching the ramp
from the ship's upper deck
she hesitates and turns
as if waiting for someone

A man approaches her
they embrace
they kiss
then separate

She slowly walks toward me
we embrace
we kiss

Years later we separate

America

I am eager to see my new adopted country
from sea to shining sea
traveling in a VW camper
feeling free

Wanting to absorb the curious new
that shocks and inspires
Seeking the spirited old
with knowledge to the source of life

Leaving the lush green New England woods
for the never seen wide and open roads
Airborne highways supported on stilts
twirling and twisting under and over each other

Massive intrusive metal structures
holding up flashy billboards
Buy me

Fleeting architecture
houses turned away from the sun
the ugly beauty of cities

America
The fertile the wasted and the wasteful

The bizarre

The powerful
The poor

The beautiful
never seen endless vistas
distant empty horizons

Theatrical skies calming
Exploding

Mountains that sing

Work

It is easy to find employment

The business of architecture is booming
educated foreigners from Europe are welcomed

My mathematical skills are challenged
changing from the metric system

I relearn the methods of design and construction
Europe uses solid masonry to build
houses here are constructed with wooden sticks

I am not attracted to the streamlined contemporary look
glass and steel
the radical new fashion
of American sixties architecture
I am drawn to preserving and restoring the old

I work for many companies
large and small
making sure not to stay too long

Restless
Searching

The Profession

Ending a long term professional partnership
I am eager to experience architecture through building
with my own hands
smelling materials
touching
getting to know them

Learn to feel the energy of places
Learn from historic structures
Learn the consciousness of matter

I am repairing abandoned buildings
that are waiting to be loved again
making use of what is there

Gutting dusty walls
covered by graffiti of lust and abuse
abandoned by poverty and ignorance
in the Hispanic neighborhood of the city
believing we can exist together

Dark wet basements
against visions of hope

The Hippy

He strums his guitar
moving his head forcefully to the beat

His scratchy voice sings
"It's the life of a Western Cowboy
moonlight and prairie combine
singing alone
rolling my own
making that cowgirl mine...."

His yodeling rings through my ears
provoking thoughts and sights of the Alps

He lives in the Goodwin building
in the center of Hartford
a desired hub for artists and musicians
His connections secure us a coveted apartment
in this creative and inspiring environment

His father was a pilot in the Air Force
Shot down
dropping bombs over Hamburg

Chief Bey

The drum is strapped to my back
while I maneuver my bicycle
through busy city streets
to the Artist Collective
in the North End of Hartford

I take drum lessons
from Chief Bey
a wise passionate master drummer from New York City

We sit in a circle
our legs lock around the wooden drums
placing wet rawhide on the opening
we enter the ritual of stringing a tight drum

We prepare for tonight's Yaboo Rite of Passage Ceremony

All drummers gather outside
in the dark rear of the hall
The Chief asks for whiskey
and washes his hands with it
he asks for marijuana
and eats it

"Listen to everyone around you
lock the beat into your body
relax in tension
let the drum play you"

Energy and emotions are high
Tonight I let the drum play me
effortless boundless bliss
one blond haired red smiling face
among all black

Change of a City

The Goodwin building raps its historic brick façade
over the distance of an entire city block
around an exterior court
open to the sky

J.P. Morgan was the owner and a tenant
after him
thousands of colorful individuals
occupied the unique apartments
patronizing shops and restaurants
coffee houses on the street level
pulsating good energy into the city's heart

Later people are evicted

Developers fill the exterior court
with a soaring high rise steel and glass tower

The sky turns black

Early 80's

For little money I buy old abandoned buildings from the city
rehabbing them into apartments
hoping for a new livelihood

Frequent notices inform me of increased interest rates
I receive constant bank demands and threats
Lawyer Fees
Creditors
There is no way to hold on

I am losing my investment
self esteem
self respect
my marriage

Pounding my anger and frustration into the innocent cushion

"FUCKING NAZIS"
"FUCKING LAWYERS"

Burned Out

I am burned out living and working in the city
Crowded apartment buildings
Nightly racket
Shouting abuses
Anger
Burglars
Violence
Sirens
Humidity
Garbage
Urine smell
Rats

The apartment building next to me burns down
I am in fire again
broken facades of smoky masonry walls
with empty holes
where glazed windows used to be

Reminders of my past

Shift of Consciousness

Hannelore introduces me to a New Age Center
hidden
in the Catskills of New York State

People are attracted to the teachings of the
beautiful
loving
Eva

I begin to change my habits of unhealthy food intake
stop smoking
stop throwing garbage around

Learning to overcome insecurities
Discovering my real self

My Core

The Hearing

I enter the Court House in Hartford

Bankrupt

Shamefully declaring my "failures" in public
Stripped of my dignity

I am allowed to keep
my accordion
drums and flute

Separation

Hannelore and I walk into the courtroom
hand in hand
holding onto each other
like brother and sister
supported by friends

We are here to divorce

The room is crowded with tension
accusing arguments

We had resolved our differences
prepared to legally let go of each other

As we are called to the stand
the judge declares smiling
" You are free as a bird"

We hug
say goodbye
and walk away
taking our memories with us

Eviction

A friend let me stay in her garden shed
an estate in the country
just big enough for a bed
a drafting table
and a wood burning stove

My hideaway lasts only one winter and one summer
until the Zoning Enforcer
fills up my doorframe with her size
flashing a camera
snapping pictures for evidence
of my illegal residency

Time to move on

The Ring

Sixteen of us
commit ourselves
to come together
four weeks
ten hours daily
to sit on the floor
in a perfect circle
and confront our fears

We trace the physical pains of our bodies
to the source of past hurts
searching through the dark tunnels
of deadened memories
freeing ourselves
with healing tears of forgiveness

Embracing Love

The Barter

I named the coffee house in the center of the city
"The Harlequin"
after a pantomime character
inherited from German comedy

On Friday and Saturday nights
the place is filled with music and poetry
beatnik poets shout out their truth
music is political and new

It is on such a creative night
I meet Mr. and Mrs. Greene
He is a retired surgeon
She owns a travel agency

They plan to venture into the restaurant business
and commission me as the architect of this project

In exchange for payment
they offer me a 40 acre parcel of wooded land
in the Berkshire hills of Western Massachusetts

My childhood vision starts to realize itself

My dream's reality begins to unfold

CHAPTER THREE

THE LAND

SENSORY CONTACT WITH NATURE

The Land

The first time I visit the land
I drive my car in anticipation
as if to see my lover

I am going to the place
I dreamed of all my life
to the hill top
where my early childhood vision
begins to transform into reality

Tumbling Autumn leaves
bounce off my windshield
celebrating excitement

The warming sun guides my way
I walk through the forest of unknown treasures
eager to offer my friendship

I lose my way
stumble
fall

It doesn't want to let me in
the walking is too hurried
my impatience too hurtful

I ask for permission to enter
listen carefully to the sounds
learn to feel the presence of things before they appear
learn to see with my eyes open and see with them closed
all my senses enter with trust and love
I walk slowly in silence
introducing myself

I feel welcome
safe
grateful

The Woods

I discover existing logging roads
overgrown by saplings
stubborn and strong
they poke my face
slap me when I least expect it
they hang on for dear life

I collect fallen wood
make use of what is on the ground
before it becomes one with the earth

I am in my dream
walking and smelling the woods
listening to the silence
gentle brushing of leaves
thunder and storms
birds singing

I let my feelings guide me to a settling place
remote from the town road
on a sloping hill
facing the sun

Under the cover of my tent

I am home

Brunhilde

When I arrive
she is waiting for me

She follows my truck
flapping her wings
half running half flying
up to the top of the hill

She greets me
nodding her head up and down
in fast excited motions

She watches all my moves
she comes close when I feed her blueberries

She is my companion

When I leave
she runs and flies
down to the road

One day she disappears
I miss Brunhilde
the Grouse

Naked

It is humid
on the breezy hilltop

Distant Thunder

Warm soothing rain starts slow
rapidly increasing
tree tops sway in anticipation

Wanting to be close to seductive Mother Nature
I run through the woods
breathing in her scent
feel the rain
cooling wind
against my naked body
my bare feet touch the ground without pain

I openly declare my love

I get bit by a tick

Lyme disease

The Circle

In order for something to live
something will have to die

Mother Nature
You leave us with our anger and grief
You make us wonder and you make us question
You leave us trapped in our ignorance

Mother Nature
Do you feel like we do
Do you challenge us because you love us
Do you really love us

Mother Nature
Why do you send us your tricks and your ticks
and all the hidden soldiers
of your endless provocations

Could not your armies march unarmed and talk to us about
Love
Peace
Compassion
Could not your soldiers be emissaries of bliss

Are your actions a punishment
for the way we treat you
Do you even know the meaning of punishment

Mother Nature
You conceal your mysteries

In order for something to live
something will have to die

Perfect Mother Nature

Simplicity

I find myself
among fellow architects
sitting in a windowless lecture hall
The topic: "Conditioning of natural air"
The facilitator strongly suggests
to seal our houses from the natural environment
let machines control and condition the air inside

On my drive home to the land
I let the wind cool my hot head
I am reminded of
millions of suffering asthma victims
and numerous related illnesses
that are directly linked
to mechanical air
pulling and pushing toxic particles
through an enclosed environment

I ache to experience the healing woods
the mysteries of nature
be part of
learn from
respect and love

The first shelter I build
is a tipi

The Tipi

The tipi is much better to live in
always clean
warm in winter
cool in summer
easy to move

The white man builds big house
cost much money
like big cage
shut out sun
can never move
always sick

Chief Flying Hawk (1852-1931)

Black Elk

I trust
when I am ready to receive
and willing to grow
my teachers will appear

This time in the form of a book
"Black Elk
The sacred ways of a Lakota"

He is a Medicine Man
teaching us
to love each other
to bring wisdom
health
help
to all life

This beautiful and hopeful philosophy feels true to me
I continue my quest
learning and adopting
the teachings of Spiritual Elders

Meditation

I touch the earth with naked feet
let nature's scent and energy flow through me

Listen to the symphony
of babbling brooks
rushing water
the silence of a star filled night

Wind blowing through tree tops
Raindrops playing percussion

Natures Music

The origin of Beauty

Vision Quest

Isolated on top of the hill
the land is calling me
to secluded healing places

I sit in silence
A blanket protects me from the cold of night

Pray upward
to the Eagle Nation

Pray downward
to the Stone People

Pray to the Four Directions

Alert to my emotions
dismissing bad thoughts
courageous in my innocence
letting go of doubt

Fears evaporate
Burdens lift

Purification

He finds the hill through dark woods
in the middle of the night

His flashlight signals through the canvas of my tipi
He announces himself
Wild Cat
a Lakota Indian

He is here to prepare and guide a sweat lodge ceremony
for purification of mind and body

In the morning we cut nearby saplings
mark 16 holes in a circle for the frame pieces
drive the saplings into the ground
bend and tie them together
forming a four foot high half dome

We cover the dome with heavy dark blankets
leaving no light inside
A flap towards the West serves as the entrance

Wood logs are carefully placed
in the center of the fire pit
to heat the skull sized stones
the fire keeper lights the fire

We pray to Tunkashila
pray to the spirits
pray to the four directions

We humbly crawl into the dark womb of the lodge
To renew
To rededicate

Waiting for Inspiration

What I know

I want to experience the process
building a small handcrafted shelter on the sloping hill of the land
using available stones and wood
Hand tools
Self sufficient
Off the grid

What I don't know

What form and shape it will take
is there a higher consciousness
replacing my ego
to guide me
work with me
play with me

What I trust

When I am ready to receive
my teachers will appear

The Sign

I browse the isles of a bookstore
there it is
at eye level

"Sacred Geometry"
by Robert Lawlor

The philosophy and practice of measuring the earth
A science of natural law
embodied in the archetypical forms of

CIRCLE
TRIANGLE
SQUARE

I am guided in a direction that I trust
feels true

Without a preconceived plan
Without the power of ego
I follow my heart
and begin the process of building my shelter

In Love

I am hopelessly in love
with the land
the process
building the shelter

Isolated
I neglect to be with my friends
forget to financially support myself

Surrounded by beauty
making the land my lover

Until I miss the human touch

The Visit

My aching bones are massaged
by the warm waters of the solar shower

I dry my eyes and notice a black blur some twenty feet away
I scramble for my glasses
He stares at me
curious
a big black bear

I freeze
he stands still in his might
I am dripping in my nakedness

We confront each other
until he decides this meeting to be worthless
shakes his head
slowly turns around
melting into the dark woods

I wonder if he is a messenger for me

The Fall

Cold winter winds and icy snowflakes bite into my face
standing on a scaffold
framing the roof of my shelter

A split moment of failed concentration
the saw's oily chain
cuts into my arm like butter

Falling feels like slow motion
the impact of the stone wall takes my breath away

Darkness

Sharp pain in my lower back
I cannot move my legs

Oh God

Delirious Shivering

I wrap my bloody arm with a towel
crawl to the nearby truck
drive down the hill
safety

Outside

My aching back
and lack of money
force me to go back
to the other world
outside the protective land

I find a job as a teacher
in the city's Art School

That is where I meet Kristin

I trust

I am ready to receive
willing to grow

My teacher appears

Working with light, or
the concept of light,
thinking of the light
helps you experience
the light within you

Best Friends

She is my student
I am her teacher

I am rescued by the wink of her eye

Thank you Kristin

You speak with your heart
your eyes

We share our stories

Painful memories of abuse
haunted by loss
alcohol and betrayal

Lasting impacts
make you strong
independent
wise and compassionate

I see your beauty
when you do not

You see my strength
when I feel weak

We share our love
our work
our hopes
our life together

She is my teacher
I am her student

Saying Goodbye

I feel restless driving my car through thick city traffic
on my way home to the healing woods

A small persistent voice urges me to turn back
I trust and follow my intuition

An urgent phone call from Hamburg

My brother is dying of cancer

I am holding a picture of him only weeks earlier
racing his bicycle through the finish line
Strong and Athletic

We talk
We cry
We say goodbye

That night he dies

Return to the Land

I am back in the arms of nature
slipping into my walking boots
stretching my legs through driving rain
leaning against the wind
smelling the aromas of wet Mother Earth

Brilliant leaves
against darkness of the forest floor
raindrops play music

It's a bountiful and beautiful October day

I am back to the land
continuing the process
building the shelter
my childhood vision

I am grateful

Charlie's Funeral

You schlepped the heavy loads of sand
fieldstones and wood
up the hill
tough and topless

You battled up and down the fearful slopes
banging your body against trees and rocks
no more fenders
no more doors
you don't look like Charlie anymore

You were there for me
with the turn of a key
You were there for me
on that winter's day of my fall

Now that your tireless engine has died
and you slowly sink into the ground

I thank you very much

Goodbye Charlie

Rebirth

I am possessed with desire for her
losing myself in weakness and rejection

On a cold rainy night
I confront my fears

Floating in the hot tub's warm womb
feeling comfortable and safe
I close my eyes
slowly breathe with concentration
letting energy flow from the top of my head
escaping through my fingers and toes
with tingling sensation

Deeply breathing in and out
letting go of
fear
doubt
possession
desire
lust

Everything is dying

My body shakes
I slowly settle into the moment
let go

I regain my strength
finding the center of trust
finding myself

Tag Sale

"Stop the Car"

We find ourselves in a colorful black neighborhood
our presence is noted with curious looks
and silent avoidance
We walk anxiously toward the treasure
waiting among many other used items
to be rediscovered and loved again

The woman selling the accordion sadly smiles
"I bought it for my son
he did not take to it
I'll sell it for $25.00"

I open the case
lift the shiny accordion
strap it around my shoulders
and play
"My eyes have seen the glory of the coming of the Lord……."
people gather around and join in the music
singing and clapping hands
we all finish with a rousing
"Glory Glory Hallelujah
the truth is marching on"

Lucky Penny

Driving home from a visit to New York
we stop for coffee
Kris picks a penny from the ground
"It's a lucky one"

As we drive over the Tappan Zee Bridge
we begin to lose our lights and power
coming to a halt in a dark cold desolated neighborhood

Shivering fearful and tired
we walk toward a flickering motel sign
past old discarded dirty mattresses
greeted at the door by a half naked man
and his growling German Shepherd
showing off his vicious teeth
through the protective iron gate

"I am not going to stay here"
We are back sitting in our cold car
late into the night

Suddenly a black face appears outside our window
he urges us to lock the doors in this dangerous neighborhood
asks if he can help
He has an errand but offers to return
to drive us back to our friends

We wait in darkness
trust

Honoring his promise
he drives us many miles back to where we started
we share stories and laughter

It was a lucky day

Sweat Lodge Ceremony

The iron gates slowly open
Two armed guards stop my truck
inspecting for possible smuggled contraband

I am supplying stones from my land
to be used in a rehabilitating sweat lodge ceremony
for the inmates of this maximum security prison

I am greeted with warm friendly smiles from Medicine Story
Slow Turtle and Wild Cat
Native American Ceremonial Masters
gentle peace and fire keepers
They introduce me to Wendell Deer with Horns
who brought a buffalo skull
used in Lakota Sweat Lodge Ceremonies

They help unload the stones
"As big and round as a human skull"

In front of the blanket covered sweat lodge
we pray to the Four Directions
Stones are carefully stacked within a pyramid of firewood
In prayer
we light the fire

The inmates arrive
"Welcome friends"
Some are experienced with a sweat lodge ceremony
others are shy and it is difficult to find their eyes
We form a circle around the fire
pass the peace pipe

Silently we strip down to our nakedness
nothing to hide
entering one by one into the darkness of the lodge
crouching in a close safe circle
we feel each others breath
The fire keeper carefully places the first stones
into the center of the lodge
"Welcome relatives"

We listen to the cracking stones
flashing fire sparks disappear into the moist air
A splash from a bucket of cold water onto the stones
transforms with a hiss into hot burning steam
biting our naked bodies
bravely breathing in
breathing out
we begin to sweat
letting go of fear
letting go of anger

The beating of the drum
sweet smell of sage
chanting to the spirits
sweating out guilt
giving it to the Universe
the Great Creator
all the good Spirits
Trust
Sweat
Let go

More hot burning stones
"Welcome relatives"
More biting steam
dripping out toxins
memories of shame
let go – let go – let go

We firmly hold the talking stick
passing from one person to the next
openly sharing our truth
listen without judgment
into the dark

Silently
we gather around the outside fire
praying for each other
hugs and encouragements
parting in peace

I give thanks to the Universe

The Outcome

I am back on the land
Seductive Mother Earth welcomes me
Tranquility

The little "Castle"
my childhood vision
is complete

For twenty-five years
I have created a safe haven
in the arms of nature
guided by spirits
to the next step
next process
next dream

CHAPTER FOUR

THE PROCESS

BUILDING A ONE THOUSAND SQUARE FOOT
SHELTER WITHOUT A PRECONCEIVED PLAN

**THANK YOU
GUIDING SPIRITS**

Fire

I learn from Native American Indians
to look for fallen ash hickory and oak trees
to build a sacred fire

I start the fire at the rise of early dawn
keeping it alive until the sun sets
and the moon glows

Mesmerized by the dancing flames
with their meditative power
shaping and forming imaginary life

Creating smoke that purifies

This is the Fire

that will help generations to come

if they use it in a sacred manner

But if they not use it well

the fire will have the power

to do them great harm

"The Sacred Pipe"

Wallace Howard Black Elk

ONE
UNITY
SEED
PERFECT CIRCLE

The center of my tipi is the initiator
The beginning of a process

Sacred fire
Source of knowledge

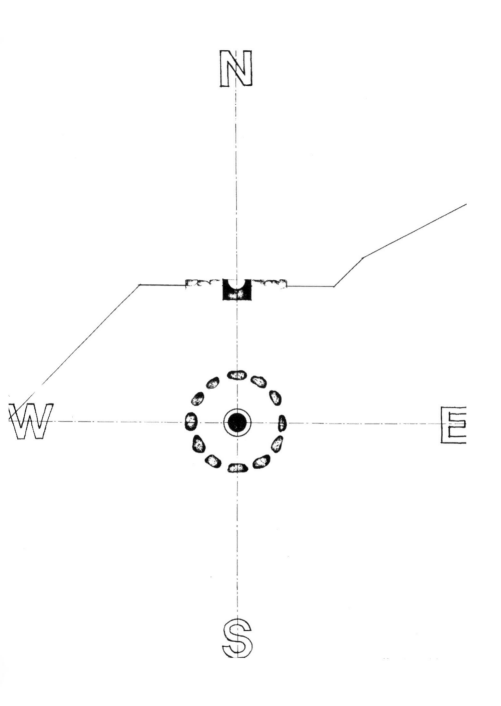

TWO
DUALITY
MULTIPLICITY

From the center of the fire pit
I orient myself to the East
placing the first found field stones into the ground

Thank you rising sun
for your illumination

I orient myself to the West
placing stones into the ground

Thank you setting sun
for your introspection

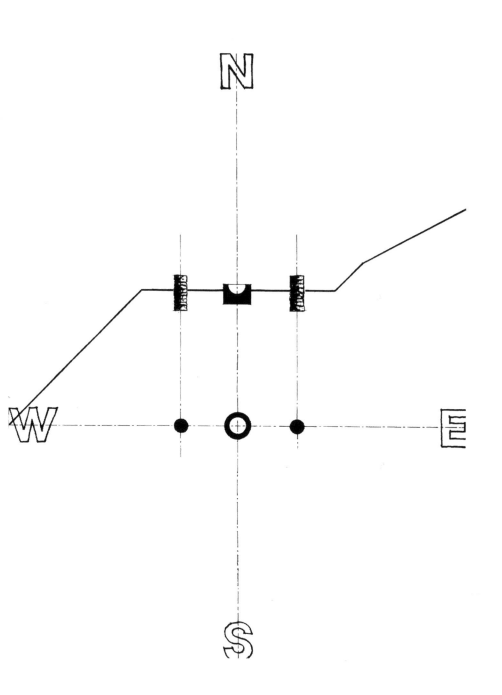

THREE
TRINITY
SURFACE
MEASURABLE

I orient myself to the North
placing the third stone foundation into the ground

Thank you moon of the night
for your wisdom

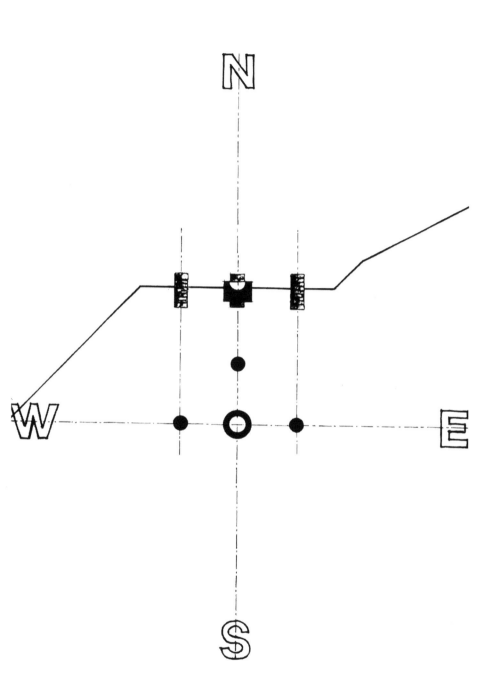

FOUR
THAT WHICH IS BORN
MATERIALIZATION
WORLD OF NATURE

I orient myself to the South
placing the fourth stone foundation into the ground

Thank you Father Sun
Fire of Life
for your trust

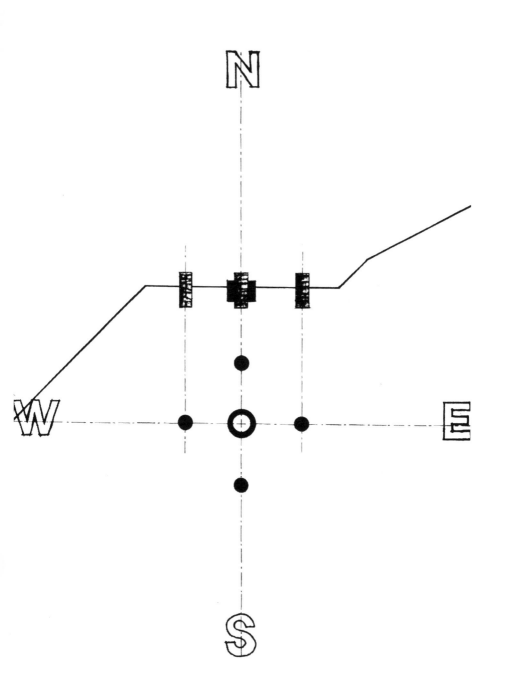

Rock

With pick and shovel
I continue carving a platform into the sloping hill
gently scarring the Earth

Stones expose themselves like potatoes
Welcome relatives

I trust your strength
your foundation

I give thanks to the Stone People

Green

While gathering wood for fuel
I improve the quality of the woodlands
collecting fallen branches
broken trees

The land will breathe better

I am grateful for the abundance

Water

In my discoveries walking the land
at the bottom of the hill
stumbling upon an unusual leaf covered heave
I find a fieldstone faced well
filled to the top
with clear fresh cold groundwater

Thank you Mother Earth
for providing this gift

Trees Talk

I wrap my naked body around its wrinkled skin
let my bare feet merge with wet earth

I feel the powerful energy
smell the scent

Communicate

Pray
Ask for permission

You give your life
for my cause

I thank you
I am grateful to you

Transformation

The nearest tree
cantilevers it's strong arms
over the center of the structure to be built
serving as a crane

Placing ropes strategically
Charlie the truck
slow and careful
pulls the twenty foot high oak tree posts
into upright positions

By wedging oak beams
into prepared openings
the trees transform into a post and beam skeleton

The spirited life of the trees continue

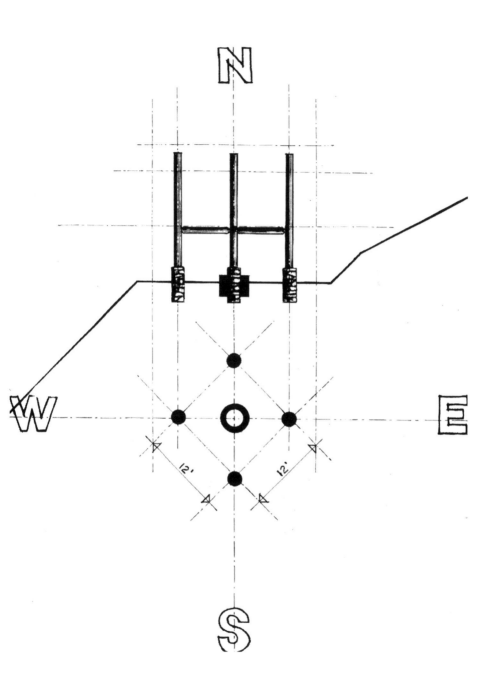

N

W

E

S

12'   12'

The Form

The structure grows from its center point

Showing me with little effort
the next steps

I celebrate

Isolated from the outside world
but not alone
in the company of guiding spirits
the shelter forms itself

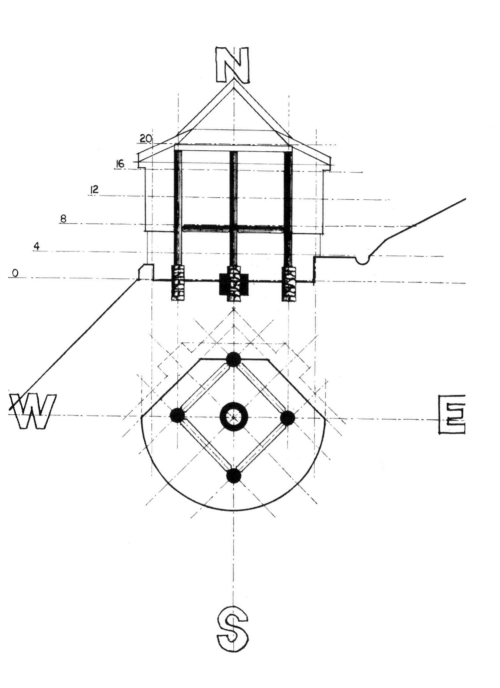

The Method

Time makes me wait
for my ego to be silent

I wait

until a gentle feeling of truth
guides me toward the next action

Directed by my requirements for space
born from the center
each form unfolds
out of a preceding one

The essential creative mystery
is rendered visible

I give thanks

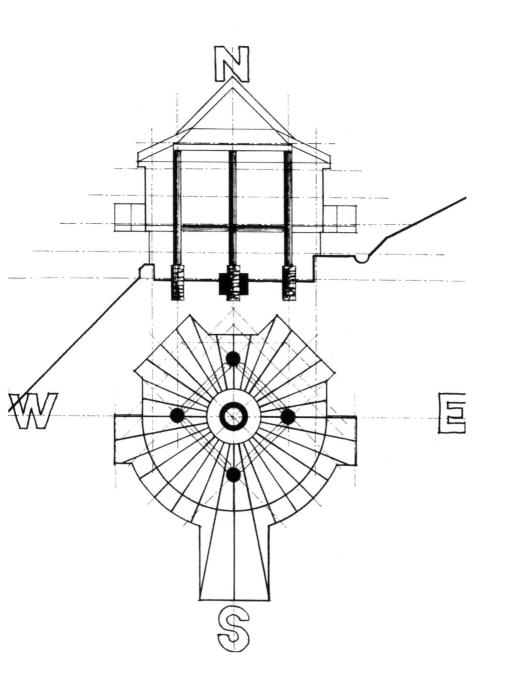

Search for systems

What are the old and tested systems
that can heat and light the shelter

What can I find on the land
to use as fuel

What are the most
simple
efficient
sustainable
technologies and materials available to me

What is the natural process
of discarding human wastes

Heat

The abundance of sticks and branches
trees broken by wind and weather
are fuel for the masonry stove

Soapstones surround a fire chamber
storing the heat
and releasing it
in a constant efficient and healthy radiation
through a brick skin

Above
sits a masonry fireplace
serving the upper level
continued by a center brick chimney
radiating heat
until it leaves the roof

The source of heat
is created in the center of the structure
as in my tipi
it is the spiritual center

I am grateful for the abundance of fuel

Light

Two photovoltaic panels
mounted on the roof
toward the South

They convert daylight
directly into electricity

Free

There is an assuring and comfortable click
coming from the distribution box
when the photovoltaic cells
charge two batteries
creating enough electric energy
for light
radio
a small refrigerator

I am grateful for the abundance of the Sun

Waste

Human and organic waste
are handled by a self-composting toilet

Nature's recycling process

Microbes break down human and organic waste
converting it back to the earth
used as compost for shrubs and flowers

Gray water from tubs and sinks
and stored rainwater
irrigate the plants

The cycle is complete

Continuation

Slowly
growing out of the center
the inside creates itself
as if devine musical harmony
allows the form
to unfreeze

An open stair winds its way around
the center masonry core

With the exception of a bathroom
there are only open areas
for cooking living and sleeping

Simple and small

It takes about one thousand steps
walking up the steep slope
to reach the shelter on the hilltop

In winter's deep snow
the steps triple

The first thousand steps
I dedicate to my early memories
The place of origin that formed me

The second thousand steps
I dedicate to my new life
The place of dreams that changed me

The third thousand steps
I dedicate to the process that lets me grow
toward a hopeful and spiritual life

Understanding
Interconnection and Responsibility
to the
Natural World
Each Other

Blessings

This story began seventy-two years ago
on the first day of an ice cold December
1938

Today is the first day of a cold December
2010

I am blessed with a long and healthy life

Sharing
my life with Kristin
her wisdom
truth
and beauty

Being
with inspirational friends
growing toward a spiritual life

Walking
the thousand steps to the top of the hill

Praying
to the spirits of the land

Collecting
wood for fuel

Erecting
my body straight up

Touching
the end of the ax with both of my hands

Swinging
the ax centered over my head

Hearing
the splitting crash of the wood log

Dancing
with naked feet to the beat of passionate drums

Playing
music that gives us gaiety and life

Seeing
the beauty in everything

Witnessing
a beautiful and hopeful change in this world

I am Blessed

Letting Go

Time to move on
to a new process
a new adventure

I have let go of the land
the house
the painful past

Walking away in love
carrying endless memories
fulfilling my dream

I am coming full circle

I am grateful to have found a new owner
who respects the sacred land
and continues to be a loving steward

In exchange
I am able to support myself
work creatively
follow my bliss

playing music of the Earth

Reflection

I will remember
your healing touch
your scent
your taste

I will remember
the intimacy of your beauty
the joy of your magic

I will remember
the awakening of your early Spring morning
standing in awe
blinded by the rays of the sun
forcing bright strokes of light
through dark trees
licking the wet ground
creating magic steam

I will remember
your luscious Summer laziness
your blooming seductiveness
your soothing warm rains

I will remember
your brilliant shining colors
your earthly scent of Autumn decay

I will remember
the frozen silence of your Winters
when the bright full moon
ever so slowly
slides in front of the sun
becoming one with each other
letting the stars light up the universe

Shining in all their glory

Not in that

he leaves something behind him,

but in that he works

and enjoys

and stirs others to work

and enjoyment,

does man's importance lie

Johan Wolfgang von Goethe

HANS LOHSE

Born 1938 near Hamburg, Germany.

He experienced the war as a young child

and was educated in construction, architecture, art and music.

He became part of Germany's angry generation

and fled to America in 1968.

He actively participates in New England communities as

an environmentally conscious registered architect,

developer and hands-on builder,

writer, musician and audio-visual artist.

He lives in Chester, Connecticut

and shares his work and life with his partner Kristin DiErrico.

8562956R0

Made in the USA
Charleston, SC
21 June 2011